W/o Theo 7522.
£2.95

The Religious Dimension of Education in a Catholic School

Vatican Congregation
for Catholic Education

CONTENTS

INTRODUCTION

1. On October 28, 1965, the Second Vatican Council promulgated the declaration on Christian education *Gravissimum Educationis*. The document describes the distinguishing characteristic of a Catholic school in this way:

"The Catholic school pursues cultural goals and the natural development of youth to the same degree as any other school. What makes the Catholic school distinctive is its attempt to generate a community climate in the school that is permeated by the Gospel spirit of freedom and love. It tries to guide the adolescents in such a way that personality development goes hand in hand with the development of the 'new creature' that each one has become through baptism. It tries to relate all of human culture to the good news of salvation so that the light of faith will illumine everything that the students will gradually come to learn about the world, about life and about the human person."[1]

The council, therefore, declared that what makes the Catholic school distinctive is its religious dimension, and that this is to be found in a) the educational climate, b) the personal development of each student, c) the relationship established between culture and the Gospel, d) the illumination of all

3

knowledge with the light of faith.

2. More than 20 years have passed since this declaration of the council. In response to suggestions received from many parts of the world, the Congregation for Catholic Education warmly invites local ordinaries and the superiors of religious congregations dedicated to the education of young people to examine whether or not the words of the council have become a reality. The second extraordinary general assembly of the Synod of Bishops of 1985 said that this opportunity should not be missed! The reflection should lead to concrete decisions about what can and should be done to make Catholic schools more effective in meeting the expectations of the church, expectations shared by many families and students.

3. In order to be of assistance in implementing the council's declaration, the Congregation for Catholic Education has already published several papers dealing with questions of concern to Catholic schools. ''The Catholic School''[2] develops a basic outline of the specific identity and mission of the school in today's world. ''Lay Catholics in Schools: Witnesses to the Faith''[3] emphasizes the contributions of lay people, who complement the valuable

4

service offered in the past and still offered today by so many religious congregations of men and women. This present document is closely linked to the preceding ones; it is based on the same sources, appropriately applied to the world of today.[4]

4. The present document restricts its attention to Catholic schools: that is, educational institutions of whatever type devoted to the formation of young people at all preuniversity levels, dependent on ecclesiastical authority and therefore falling within the competence of this dicastery. This clearly leaves many other questions untouched, but it is better to concentrate our attention on one area rather than try to deal with several different issues at once. We are confident that attention will be given to the other questions at some appropriate time.[5]

5. The pages which follow contain guidelines which are rather general. Different regions, different schools and even different classes within the same school will have their own distinct history, ambience and personal characteristics. The congregation asks bishops, religious superiors and those in charge of the schools to study these general guidelines and adapt them to their own local situations.

6. Not all students in Catholic schools are members of the Catholic Church; not all are Christians. There are, in fact, countries in which the vast majority of the students are not Catholics — a reality which the council called attention to.[6] The religious freedom and the personal conscience of individual students and their families must be respected and this freedom is explicitly recognized by the church.[7] On the other hand, a Catholic school cannot relinquish its own freedom to proclaim the Gospel and to offer a formation based on the values to be found in a Christian education; this is its right and its duty. To proclaim or to offer is not to impose, however; the latter suggests a moral violence which is strictly forbidden, both by the Gospel and by church law.[8]

I. THE RELIGIOUS DIMENSION IN THE LIVES OF TODAY'S YOUTH

1. Youth in a Changing World

7. The council provided a realistic analysis of the religious condition in the world today[9] and paid explicit attention to the special situation of young people;[10] educators must do the same. Whatever methods they employ to do this, they should be attentive to the results of

research with youth done at the local level, and they should be mindful of the fact that the young today are in some respects different from those that the council had in mind.

8. Many Catholic schools are located in countries which are undergoing radical changes in outlook and in lifestyle: These countries are becoming urbanized and industrialized, and are moving into the so-called "tertiary" economy characterized by a high standard of living, a wide choice of educational opportunities and complex communication systems. Young people in these countries are familiar with the media from their infancy; they have been exposed to a wide variety of opinions on every possible topic and are surprisingly well-informed even when they are still very young.

9. These young people absorb a wide and varied assortment of knowledge from all kinds of sources, including the school. But they are not yet capable of ordering or prioritizing what they have learned. Often enough they do not yet have the critical ability needed to distinguish the true and good from their opposites; they have not yet acquired the necessary religious and moral criteria that will enable them to remain objective and independent when faced with the

prevailing attitudes and habits of society. Concepts such as truth, beauty and goodness have become so vague today that young people do not know where to turn to find help; even when they are able to hold on to certain values, they do not yet have the capacity to develop these values into a way of life; all too often they are more inclined simply to go their own way, accepting whatever is popular at the moment.

Changes occur in different ways and at different rates. Each school will have to look carefully at the religious behavior of the young people *in loco* in order to discover their thought processes, their lifestyle, their reaction to change. Depending on the situation, the change may be profound, it may be only beginning or the local culture may be resistant to change. Even a culture resistant to change is being influenced by the all-pervasive mass media!

2. Some Common Characteristics

10. Although local situations create great diversity, there are characteristics that today's young people have in common, and educators need to be aware of them.

Many young people find themselves in a condition of radical instability. On the one hand, they live in a one-dimensional universe in which the only criterion is practical utility and the only value is economic and technological progress. On the other hand, these same young people seem to be progressing to a stage beyond this narrow universe; nearly everywhere evidence can be found of a desire to be released from it.

11. Others live in an environment devoid of truly human relationships; as a result, they suffer from loneliness and a lack of affection. This is a widespread phenomenon that seems to be independent of lifestyle: It is found in oppressive regimes, among the homeless and in the cold and impersonal dwellings of the rich. Young people today are notably more depressed than in the past; this is surely a sign of the poverty of human relationships in families and in society today.

12. Large numbers of today's youth are very worried about an uncertain future. They have been influenced by a world in which human values are in chaos because these values are no longer rooted in God; the result is that these young people are very much afraid when they think about the appalling problems in the world: the threat of

nuclear annihilation, vast unemployment, the high number of marriages that end in separation or divorce, widespread poverty, etc. Their worry and insecurity become an almost irresistible urge to focus in on themselves, and this can lead to violence when young people are together — a violence that is not always limited to words.

13. Not a few young people, unable to find any meaning in life or trying to find an escape from loneliness, turn to alcohol, drugs, the erotic, the exotic, etc. Christian education is faced with the huge challenge of helping these young people discover something of value in their lives.

14. The normal instability of youth is accentuated by the times they are living in. Their decisions are not solidly based: Today's yes easily becomes tomorrow's no.

Finally, a vague sort of generosity is characteristic of many young people. Filled with enthusiasm, they are eager to join in popular causes. Too often, however, these movements are without any specific orientation or inner coherence. It is important to channel this potential for good and, when possible, give it the orientation that comes from the light of faith.

15. In some parts of the world it might be profitable to pay particular attention to the reasons why young people abandon their faith. Often enough, this begins by giving up religious practices. As time goes on, it can develop into a hostility toward church structures and a crisis of conscience regarding the truths of faith and their accompanying moral values. This can be especially true in those countries where education in general is secular or even imbued with atheism. The crisis seems to occur more frequently in places where there is high economic development and rapid social and cultural change. Sometimes the phenomenon is not recent; it is something that the parents went through, and they are now passing their own attitudes along to the new generation. When this is the case, it is no longer a personal crisis, but one that has become religious and social. It has been called a "split between the Gospel and culture."[11]

16. A break with the faith often takes the form of total religious indifference. Experts suggest that certain patterns of behavior found among young people are actually attempts to fill the religious void with some sort of a substitute: the pagan cult of the body,

drug escape or even those massive "youth events" which sometimes deteriorate into fanaticism and total alienation from reality.

17. Educators cannot be content with merely observing these behavior patterns; they have to search for the causes. It may be some lack at the start, some problem in the family background. Or it may be that parish and church organizations are deficient. Christian formation given in childhood and early adolescence is not always proof against the influence of the environment. Perhaps there are cases in which the fault lies with the Catholic school itself.

18. There are also a number of positive signs, which give grounds for encouragement. In a Catholic school, as in any school, one can find young people who are outstanding in every way — in religious attitude, moral behavior and academic achievement. When we look for the cause, we often discover an excellent family background reinforced by both church and school. There is always a combination of factors, open to the interior workings of grace.

Some young people are searching for a deeper understanding of their religion; as they reflect on the real meaning of life they begin to find answers to their questions in the Gospel. Others have already passed through the crisis of indifference and doubt, and are now ready to commit themselves — or recommit themselves — to a Christian way of life. These positive signs give us reason to hope that a sense of religion can develop in more of today's young people and that it can be more deeply rooted in them.

19. For some of today's youth the years spent in a Catholic school seem to have scarcely any effect. They seem to have a negative attitude toward all the various ways in which a Christian life is expressed — prayer, participation in the Mass or frequenting of the sacraments. Some even reject these expressions outright, especially those associated with an institutional church. If a school is excellent as an academic institution but does not witness to authentic values, then both good pedagogy and a concern for pastoral care make it obvious that renewal is called for — not only in the content and methodology of religious instruction, but in the overall school planning which governs the whole process of formation of the students.

20. The religious questioning of young people today needs to be better

understood. Many of them are asking about the value of science and technology when everything could end in a nuclear holocaust; they look at how modern civilization floods the world with material goods, beautiful and useful as these may be, and they wonder whether the purpose of life is really to possess many "things" or whether there may not be something far more valuable; they are deeply disturbed by the injustice which divides the free and the rich from the poor and the oppressed.

21. For many young people, a critical look at the world they are living in leads to crucial questions on the religious plane. They ask whether religion can provide any answers to the pressing problems afflicting humanity. Large numbers of them sincerely want to know how to deepen their faith and live a meaningful life. Then there is the further practical question of how to translate responsible commitment into effective action. Future historians will have to evaluate the "youth group" phenomenon, along with the movements founded for spiritual growth, apostolic work or service of others. But these are signs that words are not enough for the young people of today. They want to be

active — to do something worthwhile for themselves and for others.

22. Catholic schools are spread throughout the world and enroll literally millions of students.[12] These students are children of their own race, nationality, traditions and family. They are also the children of our age. Each student has a distinct origin and is a unique individual. A Catholic school is not simply a place where lessons are taught; it is a center that has an operative educational philosophy, attentive to the needs of today's youth and illumined by the Gospel message. A thorough and exact knowledge of the real situation will suggest the best educational methods.

23. We must be ready to repeat the basic essentials over and over again so long as the need is present. We need to integrate what has already been learned and respond to the questions which come from the restless and critical minds of the young. We need to break through the wall of indifference and at the same time be ready to help those who are doing well to discover a "better way," offering them a knowledge that also embraces Christian wisdom.[13] The specific methods and the steps used to accomplish the educational philosophy of the school will therefore be condition-

15

ed and guided by an intimate knowledge of each student's unique situation.[14]

II. RELIGIOUS DIMENSION OF THE SCHOOL CLIMATE

1. What Is a Christian School Climate?

24. In pedagogical circles, today as in the past, great stress is put on the climate of a school: the sum total of the different components at work in the school which interact with one another in such a way as to create favorable conditions for a formation process. Education always takes place within certain specific conditions of space and time through the activities of a group of individuals who are active and also interactive among themselves. They follow a program of studies which is logically ordered and freely accepted. Therefore, the elements to be considered in developing an organic vision of a school climate are: persons, space, times, relationships, teaching, study and various other activities.

25. From the first moment that a student sets foot in a Catholic school, he or she ought to have the impression of entering a new environment, one illumined by the light of faith and having its own unique characteristics. The council summed this up by speaking of an environment permeated with the

Gospel spirit of love and freedom.[15] In a Catholic school everyone should be aware of the living presence of Jesus, the "master" who today as always is with us in our journey through life as the one genuine "teacher," the perfect man in whom all human values find their fullest perfection. The inspiration of Jesus must be translated from the ideal into the real. The Gospel spirit should be evident in a Christian way of thought and life which permeates all faces of the educational climate. Having crucifixes in the school will remind everyone, teachers and students alike, of this familiar and moving presence of Jesus, the "master" who gave his most complete and sublime teaching from the cross.

26. Prime responsibility for creating this unique Christian school climate rests with the teachers as individuals and as a community. The religious dimension of the school climate is expressed through the celebration of Christian values in word and sacrament, in individual behavior, in friendly and harmonious interpersonal relationships and in a ready availability. Through this daily witness the students will come to appreciate the uniqueness of the environment to which their youth has been

entrusted. If it is not present, then there is little left which can make the school Catholic.

2. Physical Environment

27. Many of the students will attend a Catholic school — often the same school — from the time they are very young children until they are nearly adults. It is only natural that they should come to think of the school as an extension of their own homes, and therefore a "school-home" ought to have some of the amenities which can create a pleasant and happy family atmosphere. When this is missing from the home, the school can often do a great deal to make up for it.

28. The first thing that will help to create a pleasant environment is an adequate physical facility: one that includes sufficient space for classrooms, sports and recreation, and also such things as a staff room and rooms for parent-teacher meetings, group work, etc. The possibilities for this vary from place to place; we have to be honest enough to admit that some school buildings are unsuitable and unpleasant. But students can be made to feel "at home" even when the surroundings are modest, if the climate is humanly and spiritually rich.

29. A Catholic school should be an example of simplicity and evangelical poverty, but this is not inconsistent with having the materials needed to educate properly. Because of rapid technological progress, a school today must have access to equipment that at times is complex and expensive. This is not a luxury; it is simply what a school needs to carry out its role as an educational institution. Catholic schools, therefore, have a right to expect the help from others that will make the purchase of modern educational materials possible.[16] Both individuals and public bodies have a duty to provide this support.

Students should feel a responsibility for their "school-home"; they should take care of it and help to keep it as clean and neat as possible. Concern for the environment is part of a formation in ecological awareness, the need for which is becoming increasingly apparent.

An awareness of Mary's presence can be a great help toward making the school into a "home." Mary, mother and teacher of the church, accompanied her son as he grew in wisdom and grace; from its earliest days, she has accompanied the church in its mission of salvation.

30. The physical proximity of the school to a church can contribute a great deal toward achieving the educational aims. A church should not be seen as something extraneous, but as a familiar and intimate place where those young people who are believers can find the presence of the Lord: "Behold, I am with you all days."[17] Liturgy planning should be especially careful to bring the school community and the local church together.

3. Ecclesial and Educational Climate

31. The declaration *Gravissimum Educationis*[18] notes an important advance in the way a Catholic school is thought of: the transition from the school as an institution to the school as a community. This community dimension is perhaps one result of the new awareness of the church's nature as developed by the council. In the council texts, the community dimension is primarily a theological concept rather than a sociological category; this is the sense in which it is used in the second chapter of *Lumen Gentium*, where the church is described as the people of God.

As it reflects on the mission entrusted to it by the Lord, the church gradually develops its pastoral instruments so that they may become ever more effective in proclaiming the Gospel and promoting total human formation. The Catholic school is one of these pastoral instruments; its specific pastoral service consists in mediating between faith and culture: being faithful to the newness of the Gospel while at the same time respecting the autonomy and the methods proper to human knowledge.

32. Everyone directly involved in the school is a part of the school community: teachers, directors, administrative and auxiliary staff. Parents are central figures, since they are the natural and irreplaceable agents in the education of their children. And the community also includes the students, since they must be active agents in their own education.[19]

33. At least since the time of the council, therefore, the Catholic school has had a clear identity, not only as a presence of the church in society, but also as a genuine and proper instrument of the church. It is a place of evangelization, of authentic apostolate and of pastoral action — not through complementary or parallel or extracurricular activity, but of its very nature: its work

of educating the Christian person. The words of the present Holy Father make this abundantly clear: "The Catholic school is not a marginal or secondary element in the pastoral mission of the bishop. Its function is not merely to be an instrument with which to combat the education given in a state school."[20]

34. The Catholic school finds its true justification in the mission of the church; it is based on an educational philosophy in which faith, culture and life are brought into harmony. Through it, the local church evangelizes, educates and contributes to the formation of a healthy and morally sound lifestyle among its members. The Holy Father affirms that "the need for the Catholic school becomes evidently clear when we consider what it contributes to the development of the mission of the people of God, to the dialogue between church and the human community, to the safeguarding of freedom of conscience." Above all, according to the Holy Father, the Catholic school helps in achieving a double objective: "Of its nature it guides men and women to human and Christian perfection, and at the same time helps them to become mature in their faith. For those who believe in Christ, these are two facets of

a single reality."[21]

35. Most Catholic schools are under the direction of religious congregations, whose consecrated members enrich the educational climate by bringing to it the values of their own religious communities. These men and women have dedicated themselves to the service of the students without thought of personal gain, because they are convinced that it is really the Lord whom they are serving.[22] Through the prayer, work and love that make up their life in community, they express in a visible way the life of the church. Each congregation brings the richness of its own educational tradition to the school, found in its original charism; its members each bring the careful professional preparation that is required by the call to be an educator. The strength and gentleness of their total dedication to God enlighten their work, and students gradually come to appreciate the value of this witness. They come to love these educators who seem to have the gift of eternal spiritual youth, and it is an affection which endures long after students leave the school.

36. The church offers encouragement to these men and women who have dedicated their lives to the fulfillment of

an educational charism.[23] It urges those in education not to give up this work, even in situations where it involves suffering and persecution. In fact, the church hopes that many others will be called to this special vocation. When afflicted by doubts and uncertainty, when difficulties are multiplied, these religious men and women should recall the nature of their consecration, which is a type of holocaust[24] — a holocaust which is offered "in the perfection of love, which is the scope of the consecrated life."[25] Their merit is the greater because their offering is made on behalf of young people, who are the hope of the church.

37. At the side of the priests and religious, lay teachers contribute their competence and their faith witness to the Catholic school. Ideally, this lay witness is a concrete example of the lay vocation that most of the students will be called to. The congregation has devoted a specific document to lay teachers[26] meant to remind lay people of their apostolic responsibility in the field of education and to summon them to participate in a common mission, whose point of convergence is found in the unity of the church. For all are active members of one church and cooperate in its one mission, even though the fields

of labor and the states of life are different because of the personal call each one receives from God.

38. The church, therefore, is willing to give lay people charge of the schools that it has established, and the laity themselves establish schools. The recognition of the school as a Catholic school is, however, always reserved to the competent ecclesiastical authority.[27] When lay people do establish schools, they should be especially concerned with the creation of a community climate permeated by the Gospel spirit of freedom and love, and they should witness to this in their own lives.

39. The more the members of the educational community develop a real willingness to collaborate among themselves, the more fruitful their work will be. Achieving the educational aims of the school should be an equal priority for teachers, students and families alike, each one according to his or her own role, always in the Gospel spirit of freedom and love. Therefore channels of communication should be open among all those concerned with the school. Frequent meetings will help to make this possible, and a willingness to discuss common problems candidly will enrich this communication.

The daily problems of school life are sometimes aggravated by misunderstandings and various tensions. A determination to collaborate in achieving common educational goals can help to overcome these difficulties and reconcile different points of view. A willingness to collaborate helps to facilitate decisions that need to be made about the ways to achieve these goals and, while preserving proper respect for school authorities, even makes it possible to conduct a critical evaluation of the school — a process in which teachers, students and families can all take part because of their common concern to work for the good of all.

40. Considering the special age group they are working with, primary schools should try to create a community school climate that reproduces, as far as possible, the warm and intimate atmosphere of family life. Those responsible for these schools will, therefore, do everything they can to promote a common spirit of trust and spontaneity. In addition, they will take great care to promote close and constant collaboration with the parents of these pupils. An integration of school and home is an essential condition for the birth and development of all of the potential

which these children manifest in one or the other of these two situations — including their openness to religion with all that this implies.

41. The congregation wishes to express its appreciation to all those dioceses which have worked to establish primary schools in their parishes; these deserve the strong support of all Catholics. It also wishes to thank the religious congregations helping to sustain these primary schools, often at great sacrifice. Moreover, the congregation offers enthusiastic encouragement to those dioceses and religious congregations who wish to establish new schools. Such things as film clubs and sports groups are not enough; not even classes in catechism instruction are sufficient. What is needed is a school. This is a goal which, in some countries, was the starting point. There are countries in which the church began with schools and only later was able to construct churches and to establish a new Christian community.[28]

4. The School as an Open Community

42. Partnership between a Catholic school and the families of the students must continue and be strengthened: not simply to be able to

deal with academic problems that may arise, but rather so that the educational goals of the school can be achieved. Close cooperation with the family is especially important when treating sensitive issues such as religious, moral or sexual education, orientation toward a profession or a choice of one's vocation in life. It is not a question of convenience, but a partnership based on faith. Catholic tradition teaches that God has bestowed on the family its own specific and unique educational mission.

43. The first and primary educators of children are their parents.[29] The school is aware of this fact, but unfortunately the same is not always true of the families themselves; it is the school's responsibility to give them this awareness. Every school should initiate meetings and other programs which will make the parents more conscious of their role and help to establish a partnership; it is impossible to do too much along these lines. It often happens that a meeting called to talk about the children becomes an opportunity to raise the consciousness of the parents. In addition, the school should try to involve the family as much as possible in the educational aims of the school — both in helping to plan these goals and

in helping to achieve them. Experience shows that parents who were once totally unaware of their role can be transformed into excellent partners.

44. "The involvement of the church in the field of education is demonstrated especially by the Catholic school."[30] This affirmation of the council has both historical and practical importance. Church schools first appeared centuries ago, growing up alongside monasteries, cathedrals and parish churches. The church has always had a love for its schools, because this is where its children receive their formation. These schools have continued to flourish with the help of bishops, countless religious congregations and laity; the church has never ceased to support the schools in their difficulties and to defend them against governments seeking to close or confiscate them.

Just as the church is present in the school, so the school is present in the church; this is a logical consequence of their reciprocal commitment. The church, through which the redemption of Christ is revealed and made operative, is where the Catholic school receives its spirit. It recognizes the Holy Father as the center and the measure of unity in the entire Christian community. Love for and fidelity to the church is the organizing principle and the source of strength of a Catholic school.

Teachers find the light and the courage for authentic religious education in their unity among themselves and their generous and humble communion with the Holy Father. Concretely, the educational goals of the school include a concern for the life and the problems of the church, both local and universal. These goals are attentive to the magisterium and include cooperation with church authorities. Catholic students are helped to become active members of the parish and diocesan communities. They have opportunities to join church associations and church youth groups, and they are taught to collaborate in local church projects.

Mutual esteem and reciprocal collaboration will be established between the Catholic school and the bishop and other church authorities through direct contacts. We are pleased to note that a concern for Catholic schools is becoming more of a priority of local churches in many parts of the world.[31]

45. A Christian education must promote respect for the state and its representatives, the observance of just

laws and a search for the common good. Therefore, traditional civic values such as freedom, justice, the nobility of work and the need to pursue social progress are all included among the school goals, and the life of the school gives witness to them. The national anniversaries and other important civic events are commemorated and celebrated in appropriate ways in the schools of each country.

The school life should also reflect an awareness of international society. Christian education sees all of humanity as one large family, divided perhaps by historical and political events, but always one in God, who is Father of all. Therefore a Catholic school should be sensitive to and help to promulgate church appeals for peace, justice, freedom, progress for all peoples and assistance for countries in need. And it should not ignore similar appeals coming from recognized international organizations such as the U.N. Educational, Scientific and Cultural Organization and the United Nations.

46. That Catholic schools help to form good citizens is a fact apparent to everyone. Both government policy and public opinion should therefore recognize the work these schools do as

a real service to society. It is unjust to accept the service and ignore or fight against its source. Fortunately, a good number of countries seem to have a growing understanding of and sympathy for the Catholic school.[32] A recent survey conducted by the congregation demonstrates that a new age may be dawning.

III. RELIGIOUS DIMENSION OF SCHOOL LIFE AND WORK

1. School Life

47. Students spend a large share of each day and the greater part of their youth either at school or doing activities that are related to school. *School* is often identified with *teaching*; actually, classes and lessons are only a small part of school life. Along with the lessons that a teacher gives, there is the active participation of the students individually or as a group: study, research, exercises, paracurricular activities, examinations, relationships with teachers and with one another, group activities, class meetings, school assemblies. While the Catholic school is like any other school in this complex variety of events that make up the life of the school, there is one essential difference: It draws its inspiration

and its strength from the Gospel, in which it is rooted. The principle that no human act is morally indifferent to one's conscience or before God has clear applications to school life: Examples of it are school work accepted as a duty and done with good will; courage and perseverance when difficulties come; respect for teachers; loyalty toward and love for fellow students; sincerity, tolerance and goodness in all relationships.

48. The educational process is not simply a human activity; it is a genuine Christian journey toward perfection. Students who are sensitive to the religious dimension of life realize that the will of God is found in the work and the human relationships of each day. They learn to follow the example of the Master, who spent his youth working and who did good to all.[33] Those students who are unaware of this religious dimension are deprived of its benefits, and they run the risk of living the best years of their lives at a shallow level.

49. Within the overall process of education, special mention must be made of the intellectual work done by students. Although Christian life consists in loving God and doing his will,

intellectual work is intimately involved. The light of Christian faith stimulates a desire to know the universe as God's creation. It enkindles a love for the truth that will not be satisfied with superficiality in knowledge or judgment. It awakens a critical sense, which examines statements rather than accepting them blindly. It impels the mind to learn with careful order and precise methods, and to work with a sense of responsibility. It provides the strength needed to accept the sacrifices and the perseverance required by intellectual labor. When fatigued, the Christian student remembers the command of Genesis[34] and the invitation of the Lord.[35]

50. The religious dimension enhances intellectual efforts in a variety of ways: Interest in academic work is stimulated by the presence of new perspectives; Christian formation is strengthened; supernatural grace is given. How sad it would be if the young people in Catholic schools were to have no knowledge of this reality in the midst of all the difficult and tiring work they have to do!

2. The School Culture

51. Intellectual development and growth as a Christian go forward hand

in hand. As students move up from one class into the next, it becomes increasingly imperative that a Catholic school help them become aware that a relationship exists between faith and human culture.[36] Human culture remains human and must be taught with scientific objectivity. But the lessons of the teacher and the reception of those students who are believers will not divorce faith from this culture;[37] this would be a major spiritual loss. The world of human culture and the world of religion are not like two parallel lines that never meet; points of contact are established within the human person. For a believer is both human and a person of faith, the protagonist of culture and the subject of religion. Anyone who searches for the contact points will be able to find them.[38] Helping in the search is not solely the task of religion teachers; their time is quite limited, while other teachers have many hours at their disposal every day. Everyone should work together, each one developing his or her own subject area with professional competence, but sensitive to those opportunities in which they can help students to see beyond the limited horizon of human reality. In a Catholic school, and analogously in every school,

God cannot be the Great Absent One or the unwelcome intruder. The Creator does not put obstacles in the path of someone trying to learn more about the universe he created, a universe which is given new significance when seen with the eyes of faith.

52. A Catholic secondary school will give special attention to the "challenges" that human culture poses for faith. Students will be helped to attain that synthesis of faith and culture which is necessary for faith to be mature. But a mature faith is also able to recognize and reject cultural counter-values which threaten human dignity and are therefore contrary to the Gospel.[39] No one should think that all of the problems of religion and faith will be completely solved by academic studies; nevertheless, we are convinced that a school is a privileged place for finding adequate ways to deal with these problems. The declaration *Gravissimum Educationis*,[40] echoing *Gaudium et Spes*,[41] indicates that one of the characteristics of a Catholic school is that it interprets and gives order to human culture in the light of faith.

53. As the council points out, giving order to human culture in the light of the message of salvation cannot

mean a lack of respect for the autonomy of the different academic disciplines and the methodology proper to them; nor can it mean that these disciplines are to be seen merely as subservient to faith. On the other hand, it is necessary to point out that a proper autonomy of culture has to be distinguished from a vision of the human person or of the world as totally autonomous, implying that one can negate spiritual values or prescind from them. We must always remember that, while faith is not to be identified with any one culture and is independent of all cultures, it must inspire every culture: "Faith which does not become culture is faith which is not received fully, not assimilated entirely, not lived faithfully."[42]

54. In a number of countries, renewal in school programming has given increased attention to science and technology. Those teaching these subject areas must not ignore the religious dimension. They should help their students to understand that positive science, and the technology allied to it, is a part of the universe created by God. Understanding this can help encourage an interest in research: the whole of creation, from the distant celestial bodies and the immeasurable cosmic

forces down to the infinitesimal particles and waves of matter and energy, all bear the imprint of the Creator's wisdom and power. The wonder that past ages felt when contemplating this universe, recorded by the biblical authors,[43] is still valid for the students of today; the only difference is that we have a knowledge that is much more vast and profound. There can be no conflict between faith and true scientific knowledge; both find their source in God.

The student who is able to discover the harmony between faith and science will in future professional life be better able to put science and technology to the service of men and women, and to the service of God. It is a way of giving back to God what he has first given to us.[44]

55. A Catholic school must be committed to the development of a program which will overcome the problems of a fragmented and insufficient curriculum. Teachers dealing with areas such as anthropology, biology, psychology, sociology and philosophy all have the opportunity to present a complete picture of the human person, including the religious dimension. Students should be helped to see the human person as a living creature hav-

ing both a physical and a spiritual nature; each of us has an immortal soul, and we are in need of redemption. The older students can gradually come to a more mature understanding of all that is implied in the concept of *person:* intelligence and will, freedom and feelings, the capacity to be an active and creative agent, a being endowed with both rights and duties, capable of interpersonal relationships, called to a specific mission in the world.

56. The religious dimension makes a true understanding of the human person possible. A human being has a dignity and a greatness exceeding that of all other creatures: a work of God that has been elevated to the supernatural order as a child of God and therefore having both a divine origin and an eternal destiny which transcend this physical universe.[45] Religion teachers will find the way already prepared for an organic presentation of Christian anthropology.

57. Every society has its own heritage of accumulated wisdom. Many people find inspiration in these philosophical and religious concepts, which have endured for millennia. The systematic genius of classical Greek and European thought has over the centuries

generated countless different doctrinal systems, but it has also given us a set of truths which we can recognize as a part of our permanent philosophical heritage. A Catholic school conforms to the generally accepted school programming of today, but implements these programs within an overall religious perspective. This perspective includes criteria such as the following:

Respect for those who seek the truth, who raise fundamental questions about human existence.[46] Confidence in our ability to attain truth, at least in a limited way — a confidence based not on feeling but on faith. God created us "in his own image and likeness" and will not deprive us of the truth necessary to orient our lives.[47] The ability to make judgments about what is true and what is false, and to make choices based on these judgments.[48] Making use of a systematic framework, such as that offered by our philosophical heritage, with which to find the best possible human responses to questions regarding the human person, the world and God.[49] Lively dialogue between culture and the Gospel message.[50] The fullness of truth contained in the Gospel message itself, which embraces and integrates the wisdom of all cultures and enriches them

40

with the divine mysteries known only to God but which, out of love, he has chosen to reveal to us.[51] With such criteria as a basis, the student's careful and reflective study of philosophy will bring human wisdom into an encounter with divine wisdom.

58. Teachers should guide the students' work in such a way that they will be able to discover a religious dimension in the world of human history. As a preliminary, they should be encouraged to develop a taste for historical truth and therefore to realize the need to look critically at texts and curricula which, at times, are imposed by a government or distorted by the ideology of the author. The next step is to help students see history as something real: the drama of human grandeur and human misery.[52] The protagonist of history is the human person, who projects onto the world, on a larger scale, the good and the evil that is within each individual. History is, then, a monumental struggle between these two fundamental realities[53] and is subject to moral judgments. But such judgments must always be made with understanding.

59. To this end, the teacher should help students to see history as a

whole. Looking at the grand picture, they will see the development of civilizations and learn about progress in such things as economic development, human freedom and international cooperation. Realizing this can help to offset the disgust that comes from learning about the darker side of human history. But even this is not the whole story. When they are ready to appreciate it, students can be invited to reflect on the fact that this human struggle takes place within the divine history of universal salvation. At this moment, the religious dimension of history begins to shine forth in all its luminous grandeur.[54]

60. The increased attention given to science and technology must not lead to a neglect of the humanities: philosophy, history, literature and art. Since earliest times, each society has developed and handed on its artistic and literary heritage, and our human patrimony is nothing more than the sum total of this cultural wealth. Thus, while teachers are helping students to develop an aesthetic sense, they can bring them to a deeper awareness of all peoples as one great human family. The simplest way to uncover the religious dimension of the artistic and literary world is to

start with its concrete expressions: In every human culture, art and literature have been closely linked to religious beliefs. The artistic and literary patrimony of Christianity is vast and gives visible testimony to a faith that has been handed down through centuries.

61. Literary and artistic works depict the struggles of societies, of families and of individuals. They spring from the depths of the human heart, revealing its lights and its shadows, its hope and its despair. The Christian perspective goes beyond the merely human and offers more penetrating criteria for understanding the human struggle and the mysteries of the human spirit.[55] Furthermore, an adequate religious formation has been the starting point for the vocation of a number of Christian artists and art critics.

In the upper grades, a teacher can bring students to an even more profound appreciation of artistic works: as a reflection of the divine beauty in tangible form. Both the fathers of the church and the masters of Christian philosophy teach this in their writings on aesthetics — St. Augustine invites us to go beyond the intention of the artists in order to find the eternal order of God in the work of art; St. Thomas sees the presence of the Divine Word in art.[56]

62. A Catholic school is often attentive to issues having to do with educational methods, and this can be of great service both to civil society and to the church. Government requirements for teacher preparation usually require historical and systematic courses in pedagogy, psychology and teaching methods. In more recent times, educational science has been subdivided into a number of areas of specialization and has been subjected to a variety of different philosophies and political ideologies; those preparing to become teachers may feel that the whole field is confused and fragmented. Teachers of pedagogical science can help these students in their bewilderment and guide them in the formulation of a carefully thought out synthesis, whose elaboration begins with the premise that every pedagogical current of thought contains things which are true and useful. But then one must begin to reflect, judge and choose.

63. Future teachers should be helped to realize that any genuine educational philosophy has to be based on the nature of the human person and

therefore must take into account all of the physical and spiritual powers of each individual, along with the call of each one to be an active and creative agent in service to society. And this philosophy must be open to a religious dimension. Human beings are fundamentally free; they are not the property of the state or of any human organization. The entire process of education, therefore, is a service to the individual students, helping each one to achieve the most complete formation possible.

The Christian model, based on the person of Christ, is then linked to this human concept of the person — that is, the model begins with an educational framework based on the person as human and then enriches it with supernatural gifts, virtues and values — and a supernatural call. It is indeed possible to speak about Christian education; the conciliar declaration provides us with a clear synthesis of it.[57] Proper pedagogical formation, finally, will guide these students to a self-formation that is both human and Christian, because this is the best possible preparation for one who is preparing to educate others.

64. Interdisciplinary work has

been introduced into Catholic schools with positive results, for there are questions and topics that are not easily treated within the limitations of a single subject area. Religious themes should be included; they arise naturally when dealing with topics such as the human person, the family, society or history. Teachers should be adequately prepared to deal with such questions and be ready to give them the attention they deserve.

65. Religion teachers are not excluded. While their primary mission must be the systematic presentation of religion, they can also be invited — within the limitations of what is concretely possible — to assist in clarifying religious questions that come up in other classes. Conversely, they may wish to invite one of their colleagues to attend a religion class in order to have the help of an expert when dealing with some specific issue. Whenever this happens, students will be favorably impressed by the cooperative spirit among the teachers; the one purpose all of them have in mind is to help these students grow in knowledge and in commitment.

IV. RELIGIOUS INSTRUCTION AND THE RELIGIOUS DIMENSION OF FORMATION

1. Nature of Religious Instruction

66. The mission of the church is to evangelize, for the interior transformation and the renewal of humanity.[58] For young people, the school is one of the ways for this evangelization to take place.[59] It may be profitable to recall what the magisterium has said:

"Together with and in collaboration with the family, schools provide possibilities for catechesis that must not be neglected.... This refers especially to the Catholic school, of course: It would no longer deserve the title if, no matter how good its reputation for teaching in other areas, there were just grounds for a reproach of negligence or deviation in religious education properly so-called. It is not true that such education is always given implicitly or indirectly. The special character of the Catholic school and the underlying reason for its existence, the reason why Catholic parents should prefer it, is precisely the quality of the religious instruction integrated into the overall education of the students."[60]

67. Sometimes there is an uncer-

tainty, a difference of opinion or an uneasiness about the underlying principles governing religious formation in a Catholic school and therefore about the concrete approach to be taken in religious instruction. On the one hand, a Catholic school is a "civic institution"; its aim, methods and characteristics are the same as those of every other school. On the other hand, it is a "Christian community," whose educational goals are rooted in Christ and his Gospel. It is not always easy to bring these two aspects into harmony; the task requires constant attention, so that the tension between a serious effort to transmit culture and a forceful witness to the Gospel does not turn into a conflict harmful to both.

68. There is a close connection, and at the same time a clear distinction, between religious instruction and catechesis or the handing on of the Gospel message.[61] The close connection makes it possible for a school to remain a school and still integrate culture with the message of Christianity. The distinction comes from the fact that, unlike religious instruction, catechesis presupposes that the hearer is receiving the Christian message as a salvific reality.

Moreover, catechesis takes place within a community living out its faith at a level of space and time not available to a school: a whole lifetime.

69. The aim of catechesis, or handing on the Gospel message, is maturity: spiritual, liturgical, sacramental and apostolic; this happens most especially in a local church community. The aim of the school, however, is knowledge. While it uses the same elements of the Gospel message, it tries to convey a sense of the nature of Christianity and of how Christians are trying to live their lives. It is evident, of course, that religious instruction cannot help but strengthen the faith of a believing student, just as catechesis cannot help but increase one's knowledge of the Christian message.

The distinction between religious instruction and catechesis does not change the fact that a school can and must play its specific role in the work of catechesis. Since its educational goals are rooted in Christian principles, the school as a whole is inserted into the evangelical function of the church. It assists in and promotes faith education.

70. Recent church teaching has added an essential note: "The basic

principle which must guide us in our commitment to this sensitive area of pastoral activity is that religious instruction and catechesis are at the same time distinct and complementary. A school has as its purpose the students' integral formation. Religious instruction, therefore, should be integrated into the objectives and criteria which characterize a modern school.''[62] School directors should keep this directive of the magisterium in mind, and they should respect the distinctive characteristics of religious instruction. It should have a place in the weekly order alongside the other classes, for example; it should have its own syllabus, approved by those in authority; it should seek appropriate inter-disciplinary links with other course material so that there is a coordination between human learning and religious awareness. Like other course work, it should promote culture,and it should make use of the best educational methods available to schools today. In some countries, the results of examinations in religious knowledge are included within the overall measure of student progress.

Finally, religious instruction in the school needs to be coordinated with the catechesis offered in parishes, in the family and in youth associations.

2. Some Basic Presuppositions

71. It should be no surprise that young people bring with them into the classroom what they see and hear in the world around them, along with the impressions gained from the "world" of mass media. Perhaps some have become indifferent or insensitive. The school curriculum as such does not take these attitudes into account, but teachers must be very aware of them. With kindness and understanding, they will accept the students as they are, helping them to see that doubt and indifference are common phenomena and that the reasons for this are readily understandable. But they will invite students in a friendly manner to seek and discover together the message of the Gospel, the source of joy and peace.

The teachers' attitudes and behavior should be those of one preparing the soil.[63] They then add their own spiritual lives and the prayers they offer for the students entrusted to them.[64]

72. An excellent way to establish rapport with students is simply to talk to them — and to let them talk. Once a warm and trusting atmosphere has

been established, various questions will come up naturally. These obviously depend on age and living situation, but many of the questions seem to be common among all of today's youth, and they tend to raise them at a younger age.[65] These questions are serious ones for young people, and they make a calm study of the Christian faith very difficult. Teachers should respond with patience and humility, and should avoid the type of peremptory statements that can be so easily contradicted.

Experts in history and science could be invited to class. One's own experiences and study should be used to help the students. Inspiration can be found in the numerous and carefully worked out responses which Vatican II gives to these kinds of questions. In theory at least, this patient work of clarification should take place at the beginning of each year, since it is almost certain that new questions and new difficulties will have come up during the vacation period. And experience suggests that every other opportune occasion should be taken advantage of.

73. It is not easy to develop a course syllabus for religious instruction classes which will present the Christian faith systematically and in a way suited

to the young people of today.

The second extraordinary general assembly of the Synod of Bishops in 1985 suggested that a new catechism be developed for the universal church, and the Holy Father immediately created a commission to begin the preparatory work on this project. When the catechism becomes available, adaptations will be necessary in order to develop course outlines that conform to the requirements of education authorities and respond to the concrete situations that depend on local circumstances of time and place.

While we await the new synthesis of Christian doctrine — the completion of the work mandated by the synod — we present by way of example an outline which is the fruit of experience. It is complete in content, faithful to the Gospel message, organic in form and is developed according to a methodology based on the words and deeds of the Lord.

3. Presentation of the Christian Message

74. As expressed by Vatican II, the task of the teacher is to summarize Christology and present it in everyday language. Depending on the level of the class, this should be preceded by a

presentation of some basic ideas about Sacred Scripture, especially those having to do with the Gospels, divine revelation and the tradition that is alive in the church.[66] With this as a base, the class begins to learn about the Lord Jesus. His person, his message, his deeds and the historical fact of his resurrection lead to the mystery of his divinity: "You are the Christ, the Son of the living God."[67] For more mature students, this study can be expanded to include Jesus as savior, priest, teacher and Lord of the universe. At his side is Mary, his mother, who cooperates in his mission.[68]

The discovery process is an important pedagogical method. The person of Jesus will come alive for the students. They will see again the example of his life, listen to his words, hear his invitation as addressed to them: "Come to me, all of you."[69] Faith is thus based on knowing Jesus and following him; its growth depends on each one's good will and cooperation with grace.

75. The teacher has a reliable way to bring young people closer to the mystery of the revealed God, to the extent that this can ever be humanly possible.[70] It is the way indicated by the Savior: "Whoever has seen me, has seen

the Father."[71] Through his person and his message we learn about God: We examine what he has said about the Father and what he has done in the name of the Father. Through the Lord Jesus, therefore, we come to the mystery of God the Father, who created the universe and who sent his Son into the world so that all men and women might be saved.[72] Through Christ we come to the mystery of the Holy Spirit, sent into the world to bring the mission of the Son to fulfillment.[73] And thus we approach the supreme mystery of the Holy Trinity, in itself and as operative in the world. It is this mystery that the church venerates and proclaims whenever it recites the Creed, repeating the words of the first Christian communities.

The process has great educational value. Its successful completion will help to strengthen the virtues of faith and of Christian religion, both of which have God as their object: Father, Son and Holy Spirit; known, loved and served in this life as we await an eternal life in union with them.

76. Students learn many things about the human person by studying science; but science has nothing to say about mystery. Teachers should help

students begin to discover the mystery within the human person, just as Paul tried to help the people of Athens discover the "unknown God." The text of John already cited[74] demonstrates that, in and through Christ, a close relationship has been established between God and each human being. The relationship has its beginning in the love of the Father; it is expressed in the love of Jesus, which led to the ultimate sacrifice of himself: "No one has greater love than this: to lay down one's life for one's friends."[75] A crowd of people constantly surrounded Jesus; they were of all types, as if representing all of humanity. As the students see this, they will begin to ask themselves why Jesus loves everyone, why he offers an invitation to all, why he gives his life for us all. And they will be forced to conclude that each person must be a very privileged creature of God to be the object of so much love. This is the point at which students will begin to discover another mystery — that human history unfolds within a divine history of salvation: from creation, through the first sin, the covenant with the ancient people of God, the long period of waiting until finally Jesus our Savior came, so that now we are the new people of God, pilgrims on earth journeying toward our eternal home.[76]

The educational value of Christian anthropology is obvious. Here is where students discover the true value of the human person: loved by God, with a mission on earth and a destiny that is immortal. As a result, they learn the virtues of self-respect and self-love, and of love for others — a love that is universal. In addition, each student will develop a willingness to embrace life and also his or her own unique vocation as a fulfillment of God's will.

77. The history of salvation continues in the church, a historical reality that is visible to the students. They should be encouraged to discover its origins in the Gospels, in Acts and in the apostolic letters; as they study these works they will see the church at its birth and then as it begins to grow and take its place in the world. From the way it comes into being, from its miraculous growth and from its fidelity to the Gospel message, the transition is made to the church as a mystery. The teacher will help students to discover the church as the people of God, composed of women and men just like ourselves, bringing salvation to all of humanity. The church is guided by Jesus, the Eter-

nal Shepherd; guided by his Spirit, which sustains it and is forever renewing it; guided visibly by the pastors he has ordained: the Holy Father and the bishops, assisted by priests and the deacons who are their collaborators in priesthood and in ministry. The church, called by God to be holy in all its members, continues to be at work in the world. This is the mystery of the one, holy, catholic and apostolic church that we celebrate in the Creed.[77]

Ecclesiology has an extremely important educational value: The ideal of a universal human family is realized in the church. As young people come to a better knowledge of the church they belong to, they will learn to love it with a filial affection; this has obvious consequences for life, for apostolate and for a Christian vision of the world.

78. As they get older, many young people stop receiving the sacraments; this may be a sign that their meaning has not been grasped. Perhaps they are seen as devotional practices for children or a popular devotion joined to a secular feast. Teachers are familiar with this phenomenon and its dangers. They will, therefore, help students to discover the real value of the sacraments: They accompany the

believer on his or her journey through life. This journey takes place within the church and therefore becomes more comprehensible as students grow in an understanding of what it means to be a member of the church. The essential point for students to understand is that Jesus Christ is always truly present in the sacraments which he has instituted,[78] and his presence makes them efficacious means of grace. The moment of closest encounter with the Lord Jesus occurs in the eucharist, which is both sacrifice and sacrament. In the eucharist, two supreme acts of love are united: Our Lord renews his sacrifice of salvation for us, and he truly gives himself to us.

79. An understanding of the sacramental journey has profound educational implications. Students become aware that being a member of the church is something dynamic, responding to every person's need to continue growing all through life. When we meet the Lord in the sacraments, we are never left unchanged. Through the Spirit, he causes us to grow in the church, offering us "grace upon grace";[79] the only thing he asks is our cooperation. The educational consequences of this touch on our relationship with God, our witness as a Chris-

tian and our choice of a personal vocation.[80]

80. Young people today are assaulted by distractions; the circumstances are not ideal for reflecting on the last things. An effective way to approach this mystery of faith is, however, available to the teacher: The Lord proposes it in his own unique way. In the story of Lazarus, he calls himself "the resurrection and the life."[81] In the parable of the rich man he helps us to understand that a personal judgment awaits each one of us.[82] In the impressive drama of the Last Judgment he points to an eternal destiny which each of us merits through our own works.[83] The good or evil done to each human being is as if done to him.[84]

81. Then, using the Creed as a pattern, the teacher can help students to learn about the kingdom of heaven: that it consists of those who have believed in him and spent their lives in his service. The church calls them *saints* even if not all are formally venerated under that title. First among them is Mary, the mother of Jesus, living a glorified life at the side of her son. Those who have died are not separated from us. They, with us, form the one church, the people of God, united in the "communion

of saints.'' Those dear to us who have
left us are alive and are in communion
with us.[85]

These truths of faith contribute
to human and Christian maturity in
several important areas. They provide a
sense of the dignity of the person as
destined to immortality. Christian hope
offers comfort in life's difficulties. We
are personally responsible in everything
we do, because we must render an account
to God.

4. Presentation of the Christian Life

82. As we have seen, each truth
of faith has educational and ethical implications,
and students should be
helped to learn about these from the
time when they first begin the study of
religion. But a systematic presentation
of Christian ethics is also needed; to
assist in this task, we present here a sample
outline.

As an introduction to a study of
the relationship between faith and life
through religious ethics, it can be helpful
to reflect on the first Christian communities,
where the Gospel message was
accompanied by prayer and the celebration
of the sacraments.[86] This has permanent
value. Students will begin to
understand the meaning of the virtue of

faith: helped by grace to give complete, free, personal and affective loyalty to the God who reveals himself through his Son.

This commitment is not automatic; it is itself a gift of God. We must ask for it and wait for it patiently. And students must be given time to grow and to mature.

83. The life of faith is expressed in acts of religion. The teacher will assist students to open their hearts in confidence to Father, Son and Holy Spirit through personal and liturgical prayer. The latter is not just another way of praying; it is the official prayer of the church, which makes the mystery of Christ present in our lives — especially through the eucharist, sacrifice and sacrament, and through the sacrament of reconciliation. Religious experiences are then seen, not as something externally imposed, but as a free and loving response to the God who first loved us.[87] The virtues of faith and religion, thus rooted and cultivated, are enabled to develop during childhood, youth and in all the years that follow.

84. The human person is present in all the truths of faith: created in "the image and likeness" of God; elevated by God to the dignity of a child of God;

unfaithful to God in original sin, but redeemed by Christ; a temple of the Holy Spirit; a member of the church; destined to eternal life.

Students may well object that we are a long way from this ideal. The teacher must listen to these pessimistic responses, but point out that they are also found in the Gospel.[88] Students may need to be convinced that it is better to know the positive picture of personal Christian ethics rather than to get lost in an analysis of human misery. In practice, this means respect for oneself and for others. We must cultivate intelligence and the other spiritual gifts, especially through scholastic work. We must learn to care for our body and its health, and this includes physical activity and sports. And we must be careful of our sexual integrity through the virtue of chastity, because sexual energies are also a gift of God, contributing to the perfection of the person and having a providential function for the life of society and of the church.[89] Thus, gradually the teacher will guide students to the idea and then to the realization of a process of total formation.

85. Christian love is neither sentimentalism nor humanitarianism; it is a new reality born of faith. Teachers

must remember that the love of God governs the divine plan of universal salvation. The Lord Jesus came to live among us in order to show us the Father's love. His ultimate sacrifice testifies to his love for his friends. And the Lord's new commandment is at the center of our faith: "This is my commandment: that you love one another as I have loved you."[90] The "as" is the model and the measure of Christian love.

86. Students will raise the standard objections: violence in the world, racial hatred, daily crime, both young and old concerned only with themselves and what they can get for themselves. Teachers cannot avoid discussing these issues, but they should insist that the commandment of Christ is new and revolutionary and that it stands in opposition to all that is evil and to every form of egoism. The new Christian ethic needs to be understood and put into practice.

87. It begins at the level of family and school: affection, respect, obedience, gratitude, gentleness, goodness, helpfulness, service and good example. All manifestations of egoism, rebellion, antipathy, jealousy, hatred or revenge must be rooted out. At the broader level

of church: a love for all that excludes no one because of religion, nationality or race; prayer for all, so that all may know the Lord; laboring together in apostolic works and in efforts to relieve human suffering; a preferential option for the less fortunate, the sick, the poor, the handicapped, the lonely. As love grows in the church, more young people may choose a life of service in it, responding to a call to the priesthood or to religious life.

As they begin to prepare for marriage: rejecting anything that would hint at a desecration of love; discovering the newness and the depth of Christian love between man and woman, including the mutuality and reserve with which it is expressed and the sincere tenderness by which it is preserved. Young people should experience love in this way from their first friendships, gradually leading to the possibility of a commitment, until finally love is consecrated for the whole of life in the sacrament of matrimony.

88. Christian social ethics must always be founded on faith. From this starting point it can shed light on related disciplines such as law, economics and political science, all of which study the human situation,[91] and this is an ob-

vious area for fruitful interdisciplinary study. But it is important to remind ourselves that God has put the world at the service of the human family.[92] As our Lord pointed out,[93] violence and injustice in society come from men and women, and they are contrary to the will of God. But in saving us, God also saves our works: A renewed world flows from a renewed heart. The works of the new Christian order of humanity are love, justice, freedom and grace.[94]

89. These, then, are the basic elements of a Christian social ethic: the human person, the central focus of the social order; justice, the recognition of the rights of each individual; honesty, the basic condition for all human relationships; freedom, the basic right of each individual and of society. World peace must then be founded on good order and the justice to which all men and women have a right as children of God; national and international well-being depend on the fact that the goods of the earth are gifts of God and are not the privilege of some individuals or groups while others are deprived of them. Misery and hunger weigh on the conscience of humanity and cry out to God for justice.

90. This is an area which can

open up broad possibilities. Students will be enriched by the principles and values they learn, and their service of society will be more effective. The church supports and enlightens them with a social doctrine which is waiting to be put into practice by courageous and generous men and women of faith.[95]

91. The guidelines developed up to this point seem excessively optimistic. While the presentation of the Christian message as "good news" is pedagogically sound,[96] the realism of revelation, history and daily experience all require that students have a clear awareness of the evil that is at work in the world and in the human person. The Lord spoke about the "power of darkness."[97] Men and women wander far away from God and rebel against the Gospel message; they continue to poison the world with war, violence, injustice and crime.

92. A teacher can invite the students to examine their own consciences. Which one of us can honestly claim to be without sin?[98] Thus they will acquire a sense of sin: the great sin of humanity as a whole and the personal sin which all of us discover within ourselves. Sin drives us away from God, rejects the message of Christ and transgresses the law of love; sin betrays con-

science, abuses the gift of freedom, offends the other children of God and harms the church of which we are all members.

93. But we are not in a hopeless situation. The teacher should help students to see, in the light of faith, that this reality has another side to it. On the world scale, the Gospel message continues to "die" as the "seed" in the soil of the earth, only to blossom and bear fruit in due season.[99] At the personal level, the Lord waits for us in the sacrament of reconciliation. It is not just a devotional practice, but rather a personal encounter with him through the mediation of his minister. After this celebration we can resume our journey with renewed strength and joy.

94. These truths can lead to a new and more mature understanding of Christianity. The Lord calls us to an endless struggle: to resist the forces of evil and, with his help, to have the courage to overpower it. This is a Christianity which is alive and healthy, at work in history and within the life of each individual.[100]

The call to be a Christian involves a call to help liberate the human family from its radical slavery to sin and therefore from the effects of sin in the cultural, economic, social and political orders. Ultimately, these effects all result from sin; they are obstacles which prevent men and women from living according to the dignity which is theirs.[101]

95. Perfection is a theme which must be part of this systematic presentation of the Christian message. To pass over it would be disloyal: to the Lord, who calls us to limitless perfection;[102] to the church, which invites us all to perfection;[103] and to the young people themselves, who have the right to know what the Lord and the church expect of them. The teacher will begin by reminding believing students that through their baptism they have become members of the church. The Christian perfection to which we are all called is a gift of Jesus through the mediation of the Spirit; but the gift requires our cooperation. Our apostolic witness must make this perfection visible in the world, today and in the future.

Once they get beyond feeling that too much is being asked of them, students will realize that perfection is actually within their grasp. The only thing they have to do is live their lives as students as well as they can:[104] Do their best in study and work; put into practice the virtues they already know in theory

— especially love, which must be lived in the classroom, at home and among friends; accept difficulties with courage; help those in need; give good example. In addition, they must find the inspiration for their daily lives in the words and the example of Jesus. They must converse with him in prayer and receive him in the eucharist. No student can say that these are impossible demands.

The ideal would be for each student to have an opportunity for spiritual guidance, to help in interior formation. It is the best way of giving orientation and completion to the religious instruction given in the classroom and, at the same time, of integrating this instruction into the personal experiences of each individual.

5. The Religion Teacher

96. The fruits of an organic presentation of the faith and of Christian ethics depend in great part on the religion teachers: who they are and what they do.

The religion teacher is the key, the vital component, if the educational goals of the school are to be achieved. But the effectiveness of religious instruction is closely tied to the personal witness given by the teacher; this witness is what brings the content of the lessons to life. Teachers of religion, therefore, must be men and women endowed with many gifts, both natural and supernatural, who are also capable of giving witness to these gifts; they must have a thorough cultural, professional and pedagogical training, and they must be capable of genuine dialogue.

Most of all, students should be able to recognize authentic human qualities in their teachers. They are teachers of the faith; however, like Christ, they must also be teachers of what it means to be human. This includes culture, but it also includes such things as affection, tact, understanding, serenity of spirit, a balanced judgment, patience in listening to others and prudence in the way they respond and, finally, availability for personal meetings and conversations with the students. A teacher who has a clear vision of the Christian milieu and lives in accord with it will be able to help young people develop a similar vision and will give them the inspiration they need to put it into practice.

97. In this area especially an unprepared teacher can do a great deal of harm. Everything possible must be done to ensure that Catholic schools have

adequately trained religion teachers; it is a vital necessity and a legitimate expectation. In Catholic schools today these teachers tend more and more to be lay people, and they should have the opportunity of receiving the specific experiential knowledge of the mystery of Christ and of the church that priests and religious automatically acquire in the course of their formation. We need to look to the future and promote the establishment of formation centers for these teachers; ecclesiastical universities and faculties should do what they can to develop appropriate programs so that the teachers of tomorrow will be able to carry out their task with the competence and efficacy that is expected of them.[105]

V. A GENERAL SUMMARY

1. What Is a Christian Formation Process?

98. The declaration of the council insists on the dynamic nature of integral human formation,[106] but it adds immediately that from a Christian point of view human development by itself is not sufficient. Education "does not merely strive to foster in the human person the maturity already described. Rather, its principal aims are these: that

as the baptized person is gradually introduced into a knowledge of the mystery of salvation, he or she may daily grow more conscious of the gift of faith which has been received."[107] What characterizes a Catholic school, therefore, is that it guide students in such a way "that the development of each one's own personality will be matched by the growth of that new creation which he or she became by baptism."[108] We need to think of Christian education as a movement or a growth process directed toward an ideal goal which goes beyond the limitations of anything human.[109] At the same time the process must be harmonious, so that Christian formation takes place within and in the course of human formation. The two are not separate and parallel paths; they are complementary forms of education which become one in the goals of the teacher and the willing reception of the students. The Gospel notes this harmonious growth in the child Jesus.[110]

99. A Christian formation process might therefore be described as an organic set of elements with a single purpose: the gradual development of every capability of every student, enabling each one to attain an integral formation within a context that includes the Chris-

tian religious dimension and recognizes the help of grace. But what really matters is not the terminology but the reality, and this reality will be assured only if all the teachers unite their educational efforts in the pursuit of a common goal. Sporadic, partial or uncoordinated efforts, or a situation in which there is a conflict of opinion among the teachers, will interfere with rather than assist in the students' personal development.

2. Educational Goals

100. The responsibility of a Catholic school is enormous and complex. It must respect and obey the laws that define methods, programs, structure, etc., and at the same time it must fulfill its own educational goals by blending human culture with the message of salvation into a coordinated program; it must help each of the students to actually become the "new creature" that each one is potentially and at the same time prepare them for the responsibilities of an adult member of society. This means that a Catholic school needs to have a set of educational goals which are "distinctive" in the sense that the school has a specific objective in mind, and all of the goals are related to this objective. Concretely, the educational

goals provide a frame of reference which:

—Defines the school's identity: In particular, the Gospel values which are its inspiration must be explicitly mentioned.

—Gives a precise description of the pedagogical, educational and cultural aims of the school.

—Presents the course content, along with the values that are to be transmitted through these courses.

—Describes the organization and the management of the school.

—Determines which policy decisions are to be reserved to professional staff (governors and teachers), which policies are to be developed with the help of parents and students, and which activities are to be left to the free initiative of teachers, parents or students.

—Indicates the ways in which student progress is to be tested and evaluated.

101. In addition, careful attention must be given to the development of general criteria which will enable each aspect of school activity to assist in the attainment of the educational objective, so that the cultural, pedagogical, social, civil and political aspects of school life are all integrated:

a) Fidelity to the Gospel as proclaimed by the church. The activity of a Catholic school is, above all else, an activity that shares in the evangelizing mission of the church; it is a part of the particular local church of the country in which it is situated and shares in the life and work of the local Christian community.

b) Careful rigor in the study of culture and the development of a critical sense, maintaining a respect for the autonomy of human knowledge and for the rules and methods proper to each of the disciplines, and at the same time orienting the whole process toward the integral formation of the person.

c) Adapting the educational process in a way that respects the particular circumstances of individual students and their families.

d) Sharing responsibility with the church. While school authorities are the ones primarily responsible for the educational and cultural activities of the school, the local church should also be involved in appropriate ways; the educational goals should be the result of dialogue with this ecclesial community.

It is clear, then, that the set of educational goals is something quite distinct from internal school regulations or teaching methods; and it is not just a description of vague intentions.

102. The educational goals should be revised each year on the basis of experience and need. They will be achieved through a formation process which takes place in stages: It has a starting point, various intermediate points and a conclusion. At each stage, teachers, students and families should determine the degree of success in achieving these goals; where there is insufficient progress they should look for the reasons and find suitable remedies. It is essential that this evaluation be seen as a common responsibility and that it be carried out faithfully.

The end of each school year is one appropriate time for such an evaluation. From a Christian perspective, it is not enough to say that this is the time for examinations. The academic program is only one part of the process, and the end of the school year is also the time for a serious and intelligent examination of which educational goals have been achieved and which have not. A much more decisive time comes at the completion of a student's years in the school, because this is the moment when students should have reached the maximum level of an education that integrates the human and the Christian.[111]

103. The religious dimension of the school climate strengthens the quality of the formation process so long as certain conditions are verified — conditions that depend both on teachers and students. It is worth noting, once again, that the students are not spectators; they help to determine the quality of this climate.

Some of the conditions for creating a positive and supportive climate are the following: that everyone agree with the educational goals and cooperate in achieving them; that interpersonal relationships be based on love and Christian freedom; that each individual, in daily life, be a witness to Gospel values; that every student be challenged to strive for the highest possible level of formation, both human and Christian. In addition, the climate must be one in which families are welcomed, the local church is an active participant and civil society — local, national and international — is included. If all share a common faith, this can be an added advantage.

104. Strong determination is needed to do everything possible to eliminate conditions which threaten the health of the school climate. Some ex-

amples of potential problems are these: The educational goals are either not defined or are defined badly; those responsible for the school are not sufficiently trained; concern for academic achievement is excessive; relations between teachers and students are cold and impersonal; teachers are antagonistic toward one another; discipline is imposed from on high without any participation or cooperation from the students; relationships with families are formal or even strained and families are not involved in helping to determine the educational goals; some within the school community are giving a negative witness; individuals are unwilling to work together for the common good; the school is isolated from the local church; there is no interest in or concern for the problems of society; religious instruction is "routine." Whenever some combination of these symptoms is present the religious dimension of the school is seriously threatened. Religious instruction can become empty words falling on deaf ears, because the authentically Christian witness that reinforces it is absent from the school climate. All symptoms of ill health have to be faced honestly and directly, remembering that the Gospel calls us to a continuous process of conversion.

105. A school exerts a great deal of effort in trying to obtain the students' active cooperation. Since they are active agents in their own formation process, this cooperation is essential. To be human is to be endowed with intelligence and freedom; it is impossible for education to be genuine without the active involvement of the one being educated. Students must act and react: with their intelligence, freedom, will and the whole complex range of human emotions. The formation process comes to a halt when students are uninvolved and unmoved. Experienced teachers are familiar with the causes of such "blocks" in young people; the roots are both psychological and theological, and original sin is not excluded.

106. There are many ways to encourage students to become active participants in their own formation. Those with sufficient knowledge and maturity can be asked to help in the development of educational goals. While they are clearly not yet able to determine the final objective, they can help in determining the concrete means which will help to attain this objective. When students are trusted and given responsibility, when they are invited to contribute their own

ideas and efforts for the common good, their gratitude rules out indifference and inertia. The more that students can be helped to realize that a school and all its activities have only one purpose — to help them in their growth toward maturity — the more those students will be willing to become actively involved.

Even students who are very young can sense whether the atmosphere in the school is pleasant or not. They are more willing to cooperate when they feel respected, trusted and loved. And their willingness to cooperate will be reinforced by a school climate which is warm and friendly, when teachers are ready to help and when they find it easy to get along with the other students.

107. One important result of religious instruction is the development of religious values and religious motivation; these can be a great help in obtaining the willing participation of the students. But we must remember that religious values and motivation are cultivated in all subject areas and indeed in all of the various activities going on in the school. One way that teachers can encourage an understanding of and commitment to religious values is by frequent references to God. Teachers learn through experience how to help the

students understand and appreciate the religious truths they are being taught, and this appreciation can easily develop into love. A truth which is loved by the teacher and communicated in such a way that it is seen to be something valuable in itself then becomes valuable to the student. One advantage of the Christological approach to religious instruction is that it can develop this love more easily in young people. The approach we have suggested concentrates on the person of Jesus. It is possible to love a person; it is rather difficult to love a formula. This love for Christ is then transferred to his message which, because it is loved, has value.

But every true educator knows that a further step is necessary: Values must lead to action; they are the motivation for action. Finally, truth becomes fully alive through the supernatural dynamism of grace, which enlightens and leads to faith, to love, to action that is in accord with the will of God, through the Lord Jesus, in the Holy Spirit. The Christian process of formation is therefore the result of a constant interaction involving the expert labor of the teachers, the free cooperation of the students and the help of grace.

108. We have already referred to

the fact that in many parts of the world the student body in a Catholic school includes increasing numbers of young people from different faiths and different ideological backgrounds. In these situations it is essential to clarify the relationship between religious development and cultural growth. It is a question which must not be ignored, and dealing with it is the responsibility of each Christian member of the educational community.

In these situations, however, evangelization is not easy — it may not even be possible. We should look to pre-evangelization: to the development of a religious sense of life. In order to do this, the process of formation must constantly raise questions about the how and the why and the what and then point out and deepen the positive results of this investigation.

The transmission of a culture ought to be especially attentive to the practical effects of that culture and strengthen those aspects of it which will make a person more human. In particular, it ought to pay attention to the religious dimension of the culture and the emerging ethical requirements to be found in it.

There can be unity in the midst of pluralism, and we need to exercise a wise discernment in order to distinguish between what is essential and what is accidental. Prudent use of the why and the what and the how will lead to integral human development in the formation process, and this is what we mean by a genuine pre-evangelization. It is fertile ground, which may at some future time be able to bear fruit.

109. In order to describe the formation process, we have had to proceed by an analysis of its various elements; this, of course, is not the way things happen in the real world. The Catholic school is a center of life, and life is synthetic. In this vital center the formation process is a constant interplay of action and reaction. The interplay has both a horizontal and a vertical dimension, and it is this qualification that makes the Catholic school distinctive from those other schools whose educational objectives are not inspired by Christianity.

110. The teachers love their students and they show this love in the way they interact with them. They take advantage of every opportunity to encourage and strengthen them in those areas which will help to achieve the goals of the educational process. Their words, their witness, their encouragement and help, their advice and friendly correction are all important in achieving these goals, which must always be understood to include academic achievement, moral behavior and a religious dimension.

When students feel loved, they will

love in return. Their questioning, their trust, their critical observations and suggestions for improvement in the classroom and the school milieu will enrich the teachers and also help to facilitate a shared commitment to the formation process.

111. In a Catholic school even this is not enough. There is also a continuous vertical interaction through prayer; this is the fullest and most complete expression of the religious dimension.

Each of the students has his or her own life, family and social background, and these are not always happy situations. They feel the unrest of the child or adolescent, which grows more intense as they face the problems and worries of a young person approaching maturity. Teachers will pray for each of them, that the grace present in the Catholic school's milieu may permeate their whole person, enlightening them and helping them to respond adequately to all that is demanded of them in order to live Christian lives.

And the students will learn that they must pray for their teachers. As they get older, they will come to appreciate the pain and the difficulties that teaching involves. They will pray that the educational gifts of their teachers may be more effective, that they may be comforted by success in their work, that grace may sustain their dedication and bring them peace in their work.

112. Thus a relationship is built up which is both human and divine; there is a flow of love and also of grace. And this will make the Catholic school truly authentic. As the years go by, students will have the joy of seeing themselves nearing maturity: not only physically, but also intellectually and spiritually. When they look back, they will realize that, with their cooperation, the educational objectives of the school have become a reality. And as they look forward they will feel free and secure because they will be able to face the new, and now proximate, life commitments.

CONCLUSION

113. The Congregation for Catholic Education asks local ordinaries and superiors of religious congregations dedicated to the education of youth to bring these reflections to the attention of all teachers and directors of Catholic schools. At the same time, the congregation wishes to affirm once again that it is fully conscious of the important service they offer — to youth and to the church.

114. Therefore, the congregation extends warm thanks to all those engaged in this work: for all they have done and for all that they continue to do in spite of political, economic and practical difficulties. For many, to continue in this

mission involves great sacrifice. The church is deeply grateful to everyone dedicated to the educational mission in a Catholic school; it is confident that with the help of God many others will be called to join in this mission and will respond generously.

115. The congregation would like to suggest that further study, research and experimentation be done in all areas that affect the religious dimension of education in Catholic schools. Much has been done, but many people are asking for even more. This is surely possible in every school whose freedom is sufficiently protected by civil law. It may be difficult in those countries which allow the Catholic school as an academic institution, but where the religious dimension leads to constant conflict. Local experience must be the determining factor in such situations; however, to the extent that it is possible, a religious dimension should always be present — either in the school or outside its walls. There has never been a shortage of families and students of different faiths and religions who choose a Catholic school because they appreciate the value of an education where instruction is enhanced by a religious dimension. Educators will know the best way to respond to their expectations, knowing that in a world of cultural pluralism dialogue

always give grounds for hope.

Rome, April 7, 1988, feast of St. John Baptist de La Salle, principal patron of teachers.

Cardinal William Baum, prefect
Archbishop Antonio M. Javierre Ortas,
secretary

Footnotes

[1] *Gravissimum Educationis*, 8.

[2] March 19, 1977.

[3] Oct. 15, 1982.

[4] From Vatican Council II: Declaration on Christian Education *Gravissimum Educationis*; Dogmatic Constitution on the Church *Lumen Gentium*; Pastoral Constitution on the Church in the Modern World *Gaudium et Spes*; Dogmatic Constitution on Divine Revelation *Dei Verbum*; Constitution on the Sacred Liturgy *Sacrosanctum Concilium*; Decree on the Apostolate of the Laity *Apostolicam Actuositatem*; Decree on Missionary Activity *Ad Gentes*; Declaration on Non-Christian Religions *Nostra Aetate*; Decree on Ecumenism *Unitatis Redintegratio*; Declaration on Religious Liberty *Dignitatis Humanae*. From Paul VI, the apostolic exhortation *Evangelii Nuntiandi* of Dec. 8, 1975. From John Paul II, the apostolic exhortation *Catechesi Tradendae* of Oct. 16, 1979; in addition, a number of his talks given to educators and to young people will be cited below. From the Congregation for Clergy, the General Catechetical Directory of April 11, 1971. All but the latter of these documents will be cited by their Latin titles in the notes which follow. In a few places, pastoral letters of bishops will be quoted.

[5] Note that the congregation has also published "Educational Guidance in Human Love: Outlines for Sex Education," Nov. 1, 1983. This theme, therefore, will receive only brief and passing mention in the present document.

[6] *Gravissimum Educationis*, 9: "It is clear that the

church has a deep respect for those Catholic schools, especially in countries where the church is young, which have large numbers of students who are not Catholics."

[7] Cf. *Dignitatis Humanae*, 2, 9, 10, 12 *et passim*.

[8] Code of Canon Law, Canon 748.2: "Persons cannot ever be forced by anyone to embrace the Catholic faith against their conscience."

[9] Cf. *Gaudium et Spes*, 4-10.

[10] Ibid., 7: "The change of mentality and of structures often call into question traditional values, especially among the young."

[11] Cf. *Evangelii Nuntiandi*, 20.

[12] Cf. Statistical Yearbook of the Church, published by the Central Statistical Office of the Church, an office within the Secretariat of State for Vatican City. By way of example, on Dec. 31, 1985, there were 154,126 Catholic schools with 38,243,304 students.

[13] Cf. 1 Cor. 12:31.

[14] Various aspects of the religious attitudes of young people developed in this section have been the object of recent statements of the Holy Father. A handy compilation of these numerous talks can be found in a book edited by the Pontifical Council for the Laity, *The Holy Father Speaks to Youth, 1980-1985*. The book is published in several languages.

[15] Cf. *Gravissimum Educationis*, 8. For the Gospel spirit of love and freedom, cf. *Gaudium et Spes*, 38: "(The Lord Jesus) reveals to us that God is love (1 Jn. 4:8), and at the same time teaches us that the fundamental rule for human perfection, and therefore also for the transformation of the world, is the new commandment of love." See also 2 Cor. 3:17: "Where the Spirit of the Lord is present, there is freedom."

[16] This question was treated in "The Catholic School," 81-82.

[17] Mt. 28:20.

[18] No. 6.

[19] Cf. the address of John Paul II to the parents, teachers and students from the Catholic schools of the Italian province of Lazio, March 9, 1985, *Insegnamenti*,

VIII/1, p. 620.

[20] Address of John Paul II to the bishops of Lombardy, Italy, on the occasion of their *ad limina* visit, Jan. 15, 1982, *Insegnamenti*, V/1, 1982, p. 105.

[21] *Insegnamenti*, VIII/1, pp. 618f.

[22] Mt. 25:40: "For indeed I tell you, as often as you have done these things to one of these least of my brothers, you have done it to me."

[23] Cf. *Perfectae Caritatis*, 8: "There are in the church a great number of institutes, clerical or lay, dedicated to various aspects of the apostolate, which have different gifts according to the grace that has been given to each: 'Some exercise a ministry of service; some teach' (cf. Rom. 12:5-8)." Also see *Ad Gentes*, 40.

[24] *Summa Theol.* II-II, q. 186, a. 1: "By antonomasis those are called 'religious' who dedicate themselves to the service of God as if they were offering themselves as a holocaust to the Lord."

[25] Ibid., a. 2.

[26] "Lay Catholics in Schools: Witnesses to the Faith."

[27] The norms of the church in this respect are to be found in Canons 800-803 of the Code of Canon Law.

[28] Cf. the address of Pope Paul VI to the National Congress of Diocesan Directors of the Teachers' Organizations of Catholic Action, *Insegnamenti* I, 1963, p. 594.

[29] Cf. *Gravissimum Educationis*, 3.

[30] Ibid., 8.

[31] A number of recent documents from national episcopal conferences and from individual local ordinaries have had the Catholic school as their theme. These documents should be known and put into practice.

[32] See, for example, the resolution of the European Parliament on freedom of education in the European community, approved by a large majority on March 14, 1984.

[33] Cf. Mk. 6:3; Acts 10:38. Useful applications of the ethics of work to the work done in school can be found in the Sept. 14, 1981, encyclical *Laborem Exercens* of John Paul II, especially in Part 5.

[34] Gn. 3:19: "By the sweat on your face shall you get

bread to eat.''

[35] Lk. 9:23: "Let him take up his cross each day."

[36] *Gravissimum Educationis*, 8: Among the elements characteristic of the Catholic school there is that of "developing the relationship between human culture and the message of salvation, so that the knowledge of the world, of life and of the human person which the students are gradually acquiring is illuminated by faith."

[37] For a description of culture and of the relationship between culture and faith, see *Gaudium et Spes*, 54ff.

[38] Cf. Denzinger-Schonmetzer, *Enchiridion Symbolorum* 3016-3017 for the traditional doctrine on the rapport between reason and faith as defined by Vatican Council I.

[39] Cf. the address of Pope John Paul II to the teachers and students of Catholic schools in Melbourne, Australia, on the occasion of his pastoral journey to East Asia and Oceania: *Insegnamenti*, Nov. 28, 1986; IX/2, 1986, pp. 1710ff.

[40] Cf. No. 8.

[41] Cf. Nos. 53-62.

[42] Pope John Paul II, speaking at the National Congress of Catholic Cultural Organizations: *Insegnamenti*, V/1, 1982, p. 131. See also John Paul II, "Letter Establishing the Pontifical Council for Culture": *Acta Apostolicae Sedis* 74 (1982), p. 685.

[43] Wis. 13:5: "Through the grandeur and beauty of the creatures we may, by analogy, contemplate their author." Ps. 19:2ff: "The heavens tell of the glory of God."

[44] Cf. Mt. 25:14-30.

[45] Cf. *Gaudium et Spes*, 12, 14, 17, 22.

[46] Ibid., 10.

[47] Cf. Denz.-Schon. 3004 for the ability to know God through human reason and 3005 for the ability to know other truths.

[48] 1 Thes. 5:21: "Examine all things, hold on to what is good." Phil. 4:8: "Everything that is true, noble or just ... let all this be the object of your thoughts."

[49] Cf. *Gaudium et Spes*, 61, on the need to hold onto certain fundamental concepts.

91

⁵⁰ Ibid., 44: At the same time there should be a vital exchange between the church and the diverse cultures of peoples.''

⁵¹ Cf. *Dei Verbum*, 2.

⁵² Cf. Blaise Pascal, *Pensees*, fr. 397.

⁵³ *Gaudium et Spes*, 37: "The whole of human history is permeated with the gigantic struggle against the powers of darkness.''

⁵⁴ Invaluable material for presenting the divine history of salvation can be found in *Lumen Gentium* and *Dei Verbum*.

⁵⁵ Cf. *Gaudium et Spes*, 62.

⁵⁶ Cf. St. Augustine, *De Libero Arbitrio*, II, 16, 42. *Patrologia Latina* 32, 1264. St. Thomas, *Contra Gentiles*, IV, 42.

⁵⁷ Cf. *Gravissimum Educationis*, 1-2.

⁵⁸ *Evangelii Nuntiandi*, 18: "For the church to evangelize is to bring the Good News to all aspects of humanity and, through its influence, to transform it from within, making humanity itself into something new.''

⁵⁹ Ibid., 44: "The effort to evangelize will bring great profit, through catechetical instruction given at church, in schools wherever this is possible and always within the Christian family.''

⁶⁰ *Catechesi Tradendae*, 69.

⁶¹ Cf. the address of Paul VI at the Wednesday audience of May 31, 1967, *Insegnamenti*, V, 1967, p. 788.

⁶² Address of John Paul II to the priests of the Diocese of Rome, March 5, 1981, *Insegnamenti*, IV/1, pp. 629f.

⁶³ Cf. Mt. 3:1-3 on the mission of the precursor.

⁶⁴ Cf. Jn. 17:9, the prayer of the Lord for those entrusted to him.

⁶⁵ Apart from strictly local concerns, these questions are generally the ones treated in university "apologetics'' manuals and are about the "preambles to the faith.'' But the questions acquire a specific nuance for today's students because of the material they are studying and the world they are living in. Typical questions have to do with atheism, non-Christian religions, divisions among Christians, events in the life of the church, the violence

and injustice of supposedly Christian nations, etc.

66 Revelation, Scripture, tradition and Christology are themes developed in *Dei Verbum, Lumen Gentium* and *Gaudium et Spes*. Study of the Gospels should be extended to include a study of these documents.

67 Mt. 16:16.

68 Concerning the Blessed Virgin Mary in the life of the pilgrim church, cf. the encyclical *Redemptoris Mater* of Pope John Paul II, 39.

69 Mt. 11:28.

70 Cf. Denz.-Schon. 2854: One cannot speak about God in the same way that one speaks about the objects of human knowledge.

71 Jn. 14:9.

72 Cf. Lk. 12:24-28; Jn. 3:16f.

73 Cf. Jn. 16:13.

74 Cf. Jn. 3:16f.

75 Jn. 15:13.

76 From the point of view of Christian anthropology, it is essential that the history of salvation presented in *Lumen Gentium* and *Gaudium et Spes* be a part of what is studied in class.

77 Important and valuable material for teaching about the church can be found in *Lumen Gentium*.

78 *Sacrosanctum Concilium*, 7: "Christ is present in the sacraments with his own authority, so that when one baptizes it is Christ himself who baptizes."

79 Jn. 1:16.

80 The content and the methods for teaching about the sacraments can be enriched through studying parts of *Lumen Gentium* and *Sacrosanctum Concilium*.

81 Jn. 11:25-27.

82 Cf. Lk. 16:19-31.

83 Cf. Mt. 25:31-46.

84 Cf. ibid. 25:40.

85 Cf. *Lumen Gentium*, Chapter 7 on the eschatological nature of the pilgrim church and its union with the heavenly church.

86 Cf. Eph. 1:1-14 and Col. 1:13-20 for doxologies which witness to the faith of the early communities. Acts

10 speaks of evangelization, conversion, faith and the gift of the Spirit in the house of the Roman official Cornelius. Acts 20:7-12 describes evangelization and the eucharist in a house at Troas.

[87] 1 Jn. 4:10: "It is not we who have loved God, but God who first loved us."

[88] Cf. Mt. 15:19f.

[89] Cf. "Educational Guidance in Human Love: Outlines for Sex Education."

[90] Jn. 15:12.

[91] Cf. *Gaudium et Spes*, 63-66 and related applications.

[92] Cf. Gn. 1:27f.

[93] Again cf. Mt. 15:19f.

[94] Cf. *Gaudium et Spes*, 93.

[95] Students should become aware of at least some of the church's major social documents.

[96] Lk. 2:10: "I bring you news of great joy."

[97] Lk. 22:53: "But this is your hour; this is the reign of darkness." Evidence of this is easily found in various abuses, acts of injustice, attacks on freedom, the overwhelming weight of misery that leads to sickness, decline and death, the scandalous inequality between rich and poor, the lack of any equity or sense of solidarity in international relations (cf. "Some Aspects of the 'Theology of Liberation'" (1984), Congregation for the Doctrine of the Faith, Introduction and Part 1).

[98] Jn. 8:7: "Let the one who is without sin cast the first stone."

[99] Cf. Lk. 8:4-15.

[100] Cf. Eph. 6:10-17, a characteristically vigorous Pauline description.

[101] Cf. the Introduction to "Some Aspects of the 'Theology of Liberation.'"

[102] Mt. 5:48: "You must be perfect as your heavenly Father is perfect."

[103] *Lumen Gentium*, 42: "All the faithful are invited and called to holiness and to perfection within their own state of life."

[104] Ibid., 39: "This holiness of the church ... is expressed in various forms according to each individual, who

in their lives and their activities join perfection to love."

[105] Some aspects of this are treated in the documents already referred to: "The Catholic School," 78-80; "Lay Catholics in Schools: Witnesses to the Faith," especially 56-59. What is said there does not apply only to the lay teachers.

[106] *Gravissimum Educationis*, 1: "Children and young people should be assisted in the harmonious development of their physical, moral and intellectual gifts.... They should be helped to acquire gradually a more mature sense of responsibility."

[107] Ibid., 2.

[108] Ibid., 8.

[109] Cf. Mt. 5:48.

[110] Lk. 2:40: "The child grew and became strong, filled with wisdom; and the favor of God was upon him." Lk. 2:52: "And Jesus grew in wisdom and stature, and in favor with God and with men."

[111] Cf. once again *Gravissimum Educationis*, 1-2.